FROM
REJECTION
TO
RELATIONSHIP
WITH GOD

FROM REJECTION TO RELATIONSHIP WITH GOD

FROM

REJECTION

TO

RELATIONSHIP

WITH GOD

LOOK TOWARD HEAVEN FOR ALL OF YOUR
HELP

YOLANDA MARSHALL

Glimpse of Glory Christian Book Publishing
P O Box 94131
Birmingham, AL 35220

ISBN: 978-0-578-04993-9

Printed in the United States of America

CONTENTS

This book is dedicated to those of you who have been rejected and feel that there is no love around you. If you have been drawn to this book, you will soon learn that God has a message He wants you to gain from the words that are profoundly expressed throughout this book. You will be encouraged, uplifted and strengthened for the rest of your life. You will have the confidence in knowing that your partnership with God will never end and that He will change your heart toward those who have rejected you. You will also learn to love God, love yourself, and love your neighbor, the importance of forgiving people, and so much more.

In Isaiah 53:3 we read, *"He is despised and rejected of men: a man of sorrows, and acquainted with grief: and we hid as it were our faces from him; he was despised, and we esteemed him not."*

Jesus was rejected before we were ever thought about being conceived. This scripture provides us with the peace in knowing that we are not alone—Jesus is always with us.

SPECIAL THANKS

To my Heavenly Father:
God, I thank you so much for continuing to pour into my life. You have given me the wisdom and knowledge to pour into the lives of your people through this gift of writing. I know that I cannot do anything without you. You have given me the courage and strength to do many things. I will continue to give you all the glory.

To my children and my grandson:
Kiarra, Marvin, and Gabriel III, thank you so much for being supportive. All of you will always hold a special place in my heart. I love each of you.

To my family:
First and foremost, I want to thank my mother, Doris, who has been such a blessing in my life. You will always be my role model. To my siblings, I want to personally thank each of you for your love, prayers and support.

To all of my friends:
I am thankful for the true friends who have always supported and encouraged me to excel in life. Rose, Latonia, and Anita, you all are very special friends who have been in my life for over twenty years.

To Peace Baptist Church in Birmingham, Alabama:
Pastor Alonzo Green Sr. and First Lady Fadrienne Green, I want to thank you all for welcoming me and my family into your ministry. Thanks to the both of you for giving me the opportunity to execute the work that God has already begun in me. I am honored to serve under your leadership. I have been truly blessed by your encouraging words.

To Victorious Church in Lithia Springs, Georgia:
Pastor Andre' K. Westfield and Elder Paula Westfield, thank you all for being a blessing in my life during the time I served under your ministry while in Georgia. I am happy to have been a part of the VC family. It was such an honor to worship and fellowship with sincere sisters and brothers in Christ who execute godly love, pray for each other, and care about doing God's business.

To my editor:
Ann Kempner-Fisher, thank you for taking the time to edit this book. I appreciate your words of encouragement, and your belief that this book will change the lives of many.

To my graphic designer at Artistic Concept:
Chris Fraser, thank you for the artwork of this awesome book cover. You were able to connect with my vision for this book cover just as you did for my first book, From Victim to Virtuous. You definitely put in the hard work to ensure that people will be drawn to this book on the bookshelves.

FROM REJECTION TO

RELATIONSHIP WITH GOD

The word rejection is defined as "the act of rejecting something."Have you ever been rejected? Who rejected you? How did it make you feel? Do you believe that you were rejected because of something you did wrong? Did you feel the need to reject others after you had experienced rejection?

It is not uncommon for any of us to experience rejection. We are often rejected by those who are very close to us—by our families, friends, and even some of our church members. Many of us have been rejected over and over again. I have learned that some people have a fear of being rejected. They do not like the feeling of being alone. When a person feels alone, it is common to reach out to others for love, support and validation. There is no need to look any further—you can reach out to God.

I have been rejected, and it did not feel good at all. The effects of being rejected pushed me right into the arms of my Heavenly Father. I have established a true, God-fearing relationship with

Him. I believe that you, too, can move from rejection to relationship with God. One songwriter says, "I've searched all over and I can't find nobody like You, Jesus." Take a look what He did for all of us.

"He is despised and rejected of men; a man of sorrows, and acquainted with grief: and we hid as it were our faces from him; he was despised, and we esteemed him not. Surely he hath borne our griefs, and carried our sorrows: yet we did esteem him stricken, smitten of God, and afflicted. But he was wounded for our transgressions; he was bruised for our iniquities: the chastisement of our peace was upon him; and with his stripes we are healed. All we like sheep have gone astray; we have turned every one to his own way; and the Lord hath laid on him the iniquity of us all. He was oppressed, and he was afflicted, yet he opened not his mouth: he is brought as a lamb to the slaughter, and as a sheep before her shearers is dumb, so he opened not his mouth" (Isaiah 53:3-7).

Jesus' suffering was well worth it. He endured so much pain and hurt. He made the sacrifice for us. We were purchased with the blood that He shed. We need to take a minute to give thanks to God. There is no one that we should ever thank more than Him.

CHAPTER 1
REJECTION IS REWARDING

"He was...rejected of men..."

(Isaiah 53:3)

Your reward is...

SALVATION

*"...****While*** *we were yet sinners, Christ died for us"* (Romans 5:8). From the moment Jesus went to the cross and died and rose from His grave, salvation was made available to all of us. Therefore, each of us has an opportunity to be saved. It was all in God's plan for Jesus' death to take place. It is so amazing to know that we have a Savior.

You can be saved if you admit that you are a sinner, repent, and *believe* that Jesus died for your sins, and then ask Him to come into your heart and be your Lord and Savior. The key word is BELIEVE. Jesus Christ is our connecting point to God. *"For I am not ashamed of the gospel of Christ: for it is the power of God unto salvation to every one that believeth"* (Romans 1:16).

There is a multitude of benefits that come with being saved. This includes joy, blessings, goodness, grace, mercy, peace, just to name a few. When you are saved, you are no longer in the dark. Because "Jesus is the light of the world," when we receive Him in our life that light is transferred to our lives. I have been saved for many years. I am truly excited about knowing that we will have everlasting life if we believe in Jesus. (Read John 6:47).

A RELATIONSHIP WITH GOD

How many of you know that having an intimate relationship with God is the best reward we can ever have? We have been afforded the opportunity to gain a relationship with our Heavenly Father through Jesus Christ. Matthew 14:6 says, "...*I am the way, the truth, and the life: no man cometh unto the Father, but by me.*"

Many people who have crossed your path may have rejected you. But God will not reject you. He will not turn you away. You can run to Him when you have been called a castaway; when you have sought help, but rejections signs were held up everywhere you went.

Now, I must say this: God rejects the things that are not of Him. But He has given us everything we need in His Holy Book to keep us on track. We might fall short of His glory sometimes. We are not perfect, but we must always remember to repent daily for our sins. We have to go to God with a pure, sorrowful heart, and He will forgive us for our transgressions with no questions asked. Unlimited forgiveness is one of those blessed benefit of having a relationship with God. He will also provide all of your needs. He will fight all of your battles. He will heal your body. He will give you favor with others. He will give you strength. He will give you wisdom. He cares about all of us.

You can call God anytime of day or night, and He will always be available to answer your prayers, dry your tears, shield your heart, and so much more. You can tell God about that situation that has been consuming most of your thinking lately. Some of you have been worrying about so many things, from how you are going to pay your rent to how you are going to get out of that abusive relationship to how you are going to make it through another day in your hostile work environment. God is saying, *"Release it to me. Give me all of your cares and concerns. I will bless you for trusting in Me."*

LOVE

God loves us unconditionally, which is why He sent His Son, Jesus, to give His life. When Jesus hung on the cross at Calvary, He said, *"Father,*

14

forgive them for they know not what they do" (Matthew 23:34). Now, that is pure love. In this scripture, it shows us that we can still love people in spite of how they treat us. You have everything if you have the love of God inside you. You must realize that you have nothing if you do not have love. Jesus said, *"But I know you, that ye have not the love of God in you. I am come in my Father's name, and ye receive me not..."* (John 5:42-43).

Because some people may not have the love of God inside of them, they will easily put conditions on their love toward others. What I mean by this is that if someone says they love you, but when you do not have money or material things(cars, jewelry, expensive clothes, etc) to give them, or you do not want to engage in any sinful acts (fornication, adultery, stealing, etc) with them, their actions are totally different toward you. You might find them using language toward you that shows no sign of love. That is not genuine (unconditional) love.

If you are a person who puts conditions on your love, God wants to renew your mind and cleanse your heart so that you can love everyone unconditionally. Matthew 22:39 says, *"...Thou shalt love thy neighbor as thyself* (this is the second great commandment)."You are exemplifying godly character when you keep His commandments, and

15

you are showing God that you love Him, too (this is the first great commandment). Deuteronomy 7:9 says, *"Know therefore that the Lord thy God, he is God, the faithful God, which keepeth covenant and mercy with them that love him and keep his commandments to a thousand generations."* It is wonderful to know that God has made this kind of agreement with those of us who love Him. It brings joy to my heart. If you agree just say, "Amen."

JOY

The Word of God says, "...*The joy of the Lord is your strength."* (Nehemiah 8:10). People who are joyful have that much needed strength to endure certain things in their life, and they tend to laugh more. You can always find something to laugh about. As a matter of fact, you should be laughing at the devil right now. He thought that he could make you feel strife when people gave up on you. He thought that he could keep you in bondage. He thought that he could make you turn your back on God. He thought that he was strong enough to keep you on his team, but you made the choice to join "the army of the Lord." You will find true happiness in God. Psalm 146:5 says, *"Happy is he that hath the God of Jacob for his help, whose hope is in the*

Lord his God." Somebody reading this book did not know that—"now you know!"

Some people will try to find happiness in other people. And because of this, they repeatedly get hurt. When God is on your side, nothing will be able to steal the joy that He gives you. So, hold your head up. You have no reason to be sad, my sister. You have no reason to be angry, my brother. You have no reason to feel ashamed. Look toward Heaven! You are now a partner with God. I want you to say this along with me, "Satan, you will not steal my joy."

PEACE

God will give you the kind of peace that transcends every obstacle that comes your way. Some people have tried to find peace in so many false remedies. We can only locate the true peace we need in Jesus Christ. There is no other remedy. There is no need to reach out to those in your circle for peace. There is no need to reach out to your job for peace. There is no need to reach out to anyone. It is time to lay prostrate before the Lord. God is saying, *"I got everything you need." "Come unto me, all ye that labour and are heavy laden and I will give you rest (peace)."*

We need peace when we do not have enough money to pay our bills. We need peace when our spouse is acting up. We need peace when our children are being disobedient. We need peace when we are feeling sick in our bodies. We will always need the peace of God in this noisy world. When you have peace, you will be able to make it through some of the toughest times in your life.

Do you remember those times you thought you were going to go crazy, and God gave you peace? When you did not have any money to buy food, and God gave you peace. When you realized your gas needle was on empty and you had to go to an important appointment, and God gave you peace. When you called your family member in a time of need and got no answer, God gave you peace. When you asked the church for assistance and they refused to help because your name was not on their roster, God gave you peace.

God wants us to trust that He will to give us peace in all matters. Roman 14:27 says, *"Peace I leave with you, my peace I give unto you: not as the world giveth, give I unto you. Let not your heart be troubled, neither let it be afraid."*

INSPIRATION FOR YOUR HEART AND SOUL:

My sister, my brother, you are a very special person to God. I want to encourage you to stay focused, stay positive, and stay in line for your reward is awesome.

PRAYER:

Lord, I thank you for offering salvation unto me through your Son, Jesus. I pray that you will continue to steer me in the right direction. I pray that your joy, peace, and love surround me everyday. In Jesus name, Amen!

THOUGHT-PROVOKING QUESTIONS

What are three things that you have experienced after receiving salvation?

    1. _____

    2. _____

    3. _____

Would you recommend salvation to any of your friends, family members, or co-workers? What approach would you take?

Do you feel that you are executing godly love on a daily basis? If not, how can you improve your love toward others?

How is your relationship with God? Do you desire to become closer to God? Would you say that this is the best relationship you have ever experienced?

How would you rate your level of joy on a scale of 1-5?

1 is weak

2 is mild

3 is average

4 is above average

5 is strong

Do you believe that you can find true peace in Jesus Christ? Have you allowed your circumstances and situations to steal your peace?

CHAPTER 2
YOU ARE REDEEMED

"...Fear not: for I {God} hath redeemed thee, I have called thee by thy name; thou art mine."

(Isaiah 43:1)

So you can...

FORGIVE YOURSELF

Are you tired of crucifying or condemning yourself for your past sins that God has already erased? People of God it is time to move forward and forgive yourself. God said, "It's over." That always settles it. It is no longer in Jesus' book. He has forgiven you. You must now release it from your mind. I know that you might be shameful for some of things you did in your past, but God is going to give you "double for your shame" (Isaiah 61:7).

Since you are on a different path in life, you can no longer give the devil or his people any place. When people attempt to hold something over your head, and they throw stones at you because of a sin you committed, please direct them to John 8:7. It says... *"He that is without sin among you, let him first cast a stone..."* This scripture highlights Jesus' response to the scribes and Pharisees (hypocrites)

22

who were adamant about stoning a woman who was caught in sin.

When Jesus addressed those who had brought this woman to Him about their sins, they left the scene one by one. We all know people like that. They are known for pointing out your faults and shortcomings, but they are blind to their own sins. We must *"forgive them, for they know not what they do."*

FORGIVE OTHERS

While some people may not be aware that they are being used by Satan when they plot and scheme against you, say hurtful things to you, put you down instead of building you up, it is always rightto forgive them. The Bible says, *"forgive one another, if any man has a quarrel (dispute, conflict) against any: even as Christ forgave you, so also ye do"* (Colossians 3:13). It will free your conscience when you forgive. We all have one. We cannot continue holding in our minds any negative images of what people have done (or said) to us. Our minds can become troubled when we refuse to forgive.

I am certain that you have heard that "forgiveness is not for you, but instead, it is for the other person." I totally agree with this statement.

Sadly, some people will hold grudges against others for years and years—even against those who have made the transition(passed away, deceased).If you are thinking, "How can someone hold a grudge that long?"The truth is that people who fail to forgive will definitely hold a grudge for a long time. I have personally heard a person say that they will not forgive an individual who wronged them when they were a child.

I want you to understand that if you are holding un-forgiveness toward anyone, it can personally stunt your growth. I do not know about you, but I want to continue to grow in every area of my life, namely, spiritually. So, if you have an unforgiving heart, do not let it continue to torment your spirit. You can experience spiritual growth if you just forgive.

Forgiving is just one way to live a fruitful {productive} life, so you certainly do not want to continue taking the route of un-forgiveness. It is not the direction to freedom, nor is it a way to stay connected to God. It is a sin and a dead end street.

STAY IN GOD'S PRESENCE

Do you want to follow God's lead? Do you like being in His presence? We have been redeemed, but we must understand the importance of staying in our Heavenly Father's presence. We believers have already been connected to Him through the blood of Jesus Christ. However, we know that sin can separate us from Him. God is forgiving, but as I stated before, "He hates sin."

There may have been a time when some of you felt disconnected from God. Have you ever thought that it could be as a result of your lifestyle, and the cycle of sin you have repeated? There were times when I did not feel close to God. I felt so apart when I was living a sinful life. I was trapped in sin and felt that there was no way out.

I soon learned that the sin (fornication)I was marinating in is what hindered me. That might even be true for you, too. There may be something you are doing that could be hindering you from moving forward in your walk with God. It is time for you to sincerely go to God in prayer and ask Him to take the desire to sin away. It has to be very personal because no one else can ever do it for you. If you have gotten away from reading the Bible on a daily basis, make sure you redirect your attention to God and feed your spirit with His book.

Once I began reading and meditating on the Word of God, it penetrated my heart. The Word of God will cleanse us, shape us, develop our character, and transform our minds. I admit at times it can be challenging and a constant battle to fight the flesh. You must realize that you are going to be tempted daily. But,1 Corinthians 10:13 says, *"There hath no temptation taken you but such as is common to man: but God is faithful, who will not suffer you to be tempted above that ye are able; but will with the temptation also make a way to escape, that ye may be able to bear it."*

By reading the Word of God you will learn that it is the best way to escape those things that have been hindering you from staying in His presence. You do not have to yield your mind, body or soul to any form of temptation. There is an exit.

Do not continue to make excuses for partaking in sinful matters. There comes a time in our life(and that time is NOW) when we must decide if we want to continue to willfully commit sin and serve Satan, or to denounce him and his works and 'get on board for Jesus,' the Master. *"For if we sin willfully after that we have received the knowledge of the truth (The Word of God), there remaineth no more sacrifice for sins"* (Hebrews 10:26).

STOP LOOKING BACK

You may have already experienced the mighty hand of God pull you out of that sinful place in your life, so you must not look back or go back. In 2 Peter 2:20-21 says, *"For if after they have escaped the pollutions of the world through the knowledge of the Lord and Savior Jesus Christ, they are again entangled therein, and overcome, the latter end is worse with them than the beginning. For it had been better for them not to have known the way of righteousness, than, after they have known it, to turn from the holy commandment delivered unto them."* This scripture has said enough for me. What about you?

There were times when many of us ran to Satan (we were enjoying every bit of sin). But God delivered us. Yet, some of us turned back and did the same thing over again. Mercy and Grace was on the scene every time! Since we have grown spiritually and studied His Word, we know that we are held accountable for our actions. We are running to God; we are dedicated and truly honored to serve Him and help to do Kingdom work. I know that it is not uncommon to look back, or even go back, especially when you are a babe in Christ, but we must remember that we have the strength of

God that will help us to resist our flesh when it tries to succumb to sin. It all starts in our mind. If we can bring our sinful minds under subjection, our flesh will fall in line every time, then we can truly "master the human experiences," of this life. Those sinful things that cause some of us to look back, and go backward, will soon cease. God can and will give us the mind that was in Christ Jesus. Believe me! We all need a Christ-like mind in order to stay committed and on the path of righteousness.

MOVE FORWARD

We must all continue to *"press toward the mark for the prize of the high calling of Christ Jesus"* (Philippians 3:14). Once we understand how important it is to please God, and all the good things He has purposed (and in store) for our lives, there wouldn't be a soul that would want to give up on their journey of life.

Therefore, we should keep "pressing on" in spite of those things that may cause us to stumble. Sure, there will be those negative things that may appear to distort that which is meant for our good. As a matter of fact, the road blocks are in position to make us quit and to hinder us from moving forward.

In order for us to move forward we must release all those negative things that happened to us in our past. We should always commit to doing what is right and focus on that which is pure and godly. I believe that if we do these things, then we will want to move forward and experience the greatness that is attached to our purpose in life.

INSPIRATION FOR YOUR HEART AND SOUL:
My sister, my brother, do not continue to beat yourself up over the mistakes that you have made in life; over the sins that you have committed. God has redeemed you from every evil work that you may have been a part of. I encourage you to continue to seek His face daily, repent, and ask Him to help you in your daily walk. He will definitely order your footsteps. Reject sin and have full confidence that God will keep you. If you are thirsty, ask God to fill your cup with righteousness.

PRAYER:
Lord, I thank you for turning my life around. I know that without having you in my life, it would be very challenging for me. I pray that you will let me feel your presence everyday. Bless me to continue to have a forgiving heart. In Jesus name, Amen!

THOUGHT-PROVOKING QUESTIONS

Have you forgiven yourself for something you did in your past? If not, why haven't you forgiven yourself?

Is there anyone you have not forgiven? If so, do you believe that you can truly move forward without forgiving that person(s)?

Do you feel as though you are in the presence of God? Do you believe that something you are doing is separating you from Him? Do you want to stay connected to God at all times?

Do you look back often over your life and beat yourself up for something you did wrong? Do you like living in the past? What steps are you taking to change?

Do you really want to move forward? Do you believe that God has something in store for you? What steps are you taking to move forward?

CHAPTER 3
YOU ARE THE REMNANT

"...I will cause the remnant...to possess all these things."
(Zechariah 8:12)

And you are...

IMPORTANT TO GOD

Someone may have called you a reject, a bomb, a fool, retarded, crazy, slow, nobody and dumb. I am certain that you were hurt by those negative words that were used to describe you. Oftentimes, what people say to us can definitely consume much of our thinking in a day. Usually the negative things that are said to us are often thought upon longer than the positive things that are said to us.

You do not have to create a negative image of yourself based upon the thoughts and words of someone else. You can create a positive image of yourself based upon the thoughts and words of God. God sees you differently than some of your family members, so-called friends, co-workers, and even some of your church members. God has identified you as His beautiful creation. You should be glad about that.

A TESTIMONY

Although you were rejected by people, you saw hope in your situation (and not everyone does). You may have lost everything you had, and every door was closed in your face. You may have had to sleep in your car. You may have even slept under a bridge. Some of you have gone from shelter to shelter. You have experienced sickness. Your finances were all messed up. At one point in your life, you thought about giving up. But you heard about God. A man or woman of God shared the gospel (good news) with you. That person did not only minister to you, but they told you that God loves you. They prayed with you, encouraged you, and helped you.

You are on the glorious side of the storm. You see the salvation of our Lord and Savior. You can hear that still small voice clearly saying, *"It was I who delivered you; It was I who filled you with the power of the Holy Ghost; I'll receive you when none one else does; I'm going to reward you for your obedience and faithfulness."* You can go ahead and shout Hallelujah! You are in the harvest season.

You have a story to tell everywhere you go..."*It was Almighty God who brought me out of bondage. It was God who gave me shelter when I was homeless. It was God who healed my body. It was God who fed me when I was hungry. It was God who clothed me when I was naked. It was God who received me in His arms."*

God is going to use you to help someone else. You can tell them about the goodness of our Heavenly Father. I strongly believe that we all go through certain things in life (and that may include being rejected) so that we can help our neighbor (all of mankind). We cannot be afraid to share our testimonies because it gives others the hope in knowing they can be delivered and experience greatness, too.

A CHOSEN VESSEL (AMBASSADOR) FOR GOD

From the beginning of creation God already had you in mind to master the task at hand. Yes, in spite of what you have gone through. Think about it. Jesus was handpicked by God to carry out an extraordinary task. Jesus was hated for everything He did (and you will be hated, too), whether it was healing the sick, casting out demons, preaching to the broken-hearted and the masses, setting the captives free, and feeding the hungry. They did everything imaginable to harm Him, from piercing His side to sticking thorns in His head. He was treated so horribly. But wait a minute, people of God—it was not bad after all—He bore the pain and hurt for all of us.

God has also chosen each of us to carry out a special kind of task. Remember, everyone will not understand your mission. They will judge you, and they will talk about you. The reason some people want be able to understand your mission is because they are too focused on 'status quo.' Don't worry! You must understand that God is rapidly shifting gears—the remnant (the remaining, the rejected) is being transitioned to leadership roles. "You have been picked out to be picked on." You have been picked on for many years, but you have also been picked out for God's use. And this happened before it was ever revealed to you. He wants to channel His power through you, man of God, and woman of God.

Like Joseph, the son of Jacob, who had eleven brothers, was a chosen vessel. Joseph, although the youngest, had the glory of God on him! His brothers hated him after he shared the dream with them that he would reign over them. The Bible says that they envied him. They picked on him, conspired against him, and cast him into a pit. They even made it look like he had been devoured by an evil beast. After they cast him into the pit, they sold him to the

Ishmaelite for twenty pieces of silver. He was taken to Egypt, but when he got there he already had favor with Pharaoh, and the servants (Read more about this story in Genesis Chapter 37).

After it was all said and done, Joseph reigned over his brothers. He was able to boldly tell them, "You meant it for my bad, but God meant it for my good." You too will soon be able to tell those who set up traps for you, cast you in a pit, and spoke evil against you, the same thing Joseph told his kindred. Sadly, his enemies were in the same blood line. How many of you have experienced the worst from members of your family? Micah 7:6 says, "...A *man's enemies are then men of his own house.*"

Joseph's brothers did not know that they were pushing him into his destiny. So, you should not be alarmed when you find out that your family is against you. Don't be alarmed when you find out that your co-workers are against you. Don't be alarmed when you find out that some of the church members are against you. It is all in God's plan. There is something special about you. The glory of God is on your life. Some people do not quite understand your essence, and they never will. What is amazing is that you did not initially choose God—He chose you. He had already anointed, appointed, and called you to do great things in His Kingdom. He has filled you with many gifts.

GIFTED

He has imparted spiritual gifts in each of us. These gifts are supposed to be used for His glory. These gifts also come without repentance (Romans 11:29). Sadly, some people will literally make a mockery of your gifts. Has someone ever made a mockery of the spiritual gifts you possess and how God is using you with those gifts? Jesus did. Joseph did. I have even experienced someone making a mockery of a spiritual gift that God has given to me. There are so many other women and men of God who are filled with spiritual gifts that have experienced some sort of criticism.

We all know that Jesus did so many wonderful things. He was despised by so many people. He would speak a Word, and it was made so. I want to briefly share one of His power working miracles mentioned in the Bible. I will direct you to the story about Lazarus (Mary's brother). Lazarus was sick and had died, and then buried, but Jesus referred to Lazarus' death as sleep. He told His disciples that Lazarus was asleep but He was going to wake Him. He also said, *"This sickness is not unto death, but for the glory of God, that the Son of God might be glorified thereby."* When Jesus arrived on the scene, He spoke a Word, *"Lazarus, come forth..."* (John 11:43). Now, that is power! Everything He did brought honor and glory to our Heavenly Father.

Joseph was a gifted man of God. He had dreams, and he could interpret them by the Spirit of God. His brothers could not handle the fact that he was gifted and would eventually be their leader. When his brothers spotted him coming toward them, they said, "Behold, this dreamer cometh." It is amazing how people view gifted people of God. Jealousy, hatred and envy can thwart people from having the love they should have toward one another.

It is so foul, immature and ignorant when a person or a group of people are so hateful toward a gifted man or woman of God. I had an encounter with an individual who needed serious help. This person had experienced rejection after rejection. Since I was familiar with being rejected, I felt led to reach out to this person, and offered to pray. Seemingly, there was no way to penetrate this person's heart—not even through prayer. This individual rejected the laying on of hands. So, I stood a few feet away and prayed, but upon the sound of my voice, this individual immediately said, "Stop saying that. You are crazy. That is of the devil when someone speaks in an unknown language. That is not God."

I could only direct this person to the Word of God. I told this individual that their thoughts about someone being filled with the Holy Ghost were contrary to the Word of God which says, *"There are diversities of gifts, but the same Spirit! And there are differences of administrations, but the same Lord. And there are diversities of operations, but it is the same God which worketh all in all. But the manifestation of the Spirit is given to every man to profit withal. For to one is given by the Spirit the word of wisdom; to another the word of knowledge by the same Spirit: To another faith by the same Spirit; to another the gifts of healing by the same Spirit; To another the working of miracles; to another prophecy; to another discerning of spirits; to another divers kinds of tongues; to another interpretation of tongues; But all these worketh that one and the selfsame Spirit, dividing to every man severally as he wills"*(1 Corinthians 12:4-11).

When God has gifted someone with diver's kinds of tongues, that person does not know what they are saying; it is Jesus interceding on our behalf. It is hard for some people to fathom that. Some people are far away from God, but not too far to where He cannot reach them—but not by force. If someone desires a relationship with God, He will not deny them. But when someone denies God and who He has chosen to help them to become mentally, emotionally, socially and spiritually free, then we must shake the dust off our feet and continue to move on.

When God sent His disciples (gifted men of God)out in pairs, He told them, *"Go into the way of the Gentiles and into the city of Samaritans enter ye not: But go rather to the lost sheep of the house of Israel. And as ye go, preach, saying, the kingdom of heaven is at hand. Heal the sick, cleanse the lepers, and raise the dead, cast out devils: freely ye have received, freely give. Provide neither gold, nor silver nor brass in your purses, nor scrip for your journey, neither two coasts, neither shoes, nor yet staves: for the workman is worthy of his meat. And into whatsoever city or town shall ye enquire who in it is worthy; and there abide till ye go thence. And when ye come into a house, salute it. And if the house be worthy, let your peace come upon it: but if it be not worthy, let your peace return to you. And whosoever shall not receive you (the gift of healing, wisdom, understanding...), nor hear your words, when ye depart out of that house or city, shake off the dust of your feet"* (Matthew 10:5-14). People of God, if you are operating in one of these gifts mentioned in the

40

Bible, know that everyone will not receive you. That is perfectly fine.

INSPIRATION FOR YOUR HEART AND SOUL:
My sister, my brother, you do not have to ponder on why you have been picked on, why people do not want to come around you, why people rejected you...God has you. You were already picked out by Him for a time such as now. He is getting ready to use you in a mighty way. You can believe that with your heart and soul. And because you have sought the kingdom of God, all these things (natural and spiritual) have been added unto you.

PRAYER:
Lord, I thank you for seeing me differently than how others have seen me. I thank you for filling me with your gifts. I thank you for preparing me for what is ahead of me. I pray that you will continue to use me for your glory. In Jesus name, Amen!

THOUGHT-PROVOKING QUESTIONS

How important do you feel that you are to God? Has anyone ever made you feel less than God's best? How do you think God looks at you? Do you care about what God thinks of you, or what people think of you?

Do you have a testimony? If so, are you ashamed to share it with others? Do you believe that your testimony can help others? If so, in what ways do you believe it can help others?

Do you believe that you are an ambassador for Jesus Christ? Do you enjoy witnessing to the lost souls? Are you amazed that God has chosen you to execute a certain task that seems too complicated for others to carry out?

Do you possess any spiritual gifts? If so, what are they? Have you been seeking God for other gifts? Do you want your gifts to evolve?

CHAPTER 4
YOU ARE A MOUNTAIN MOVER

"...If ye have faith as a grain of a mustard seed, ye shall ay unto this mountain, Remove hence to yonder place..."
(Matthew 17:20)

You just...

HAVE FAITH

The beauty of how faith works is awesome. And the power of what it can do is amazing. Everything has to line up in your life when you have faith in God. By trusting Him in the process of your faith walk, you shall see Him move in your life. He will always honor His Word. It will not return unto Him void (Isaiah 55:11).

When your belief in God and faith are joined together, you will see the manifestation of the hand works of Him. He is always working full-time behind the scene for each of us, and He will show up on the scene when we need Him. With God on our side, we will be able to move the mountain—anything that is standing in our way has to go when we have *"the faith as a grain of a mustard seed..."* If you are

44

facing a challenging situation right now, your faith can change it. Yes, it truly can.

When I read the story about Shadrach, Meshach, and Abednego that can be found in the Book of Daniel, Chapter 3—some people might refer to these men as "The Hebrew Boys." I learned that their faith in God changed their situation. These men were faced with a serious dilemma. When King Nebuchadnezzar made a false image of God, he commanded that every man bow down and worship the image upon the sound of the music. Well, "The Hebrew Boys" did not bow down. They told the king, *"We are not careful to answer thee in this matter, but if it be so, our God whom we serve is able to deliver us from the burning fiery furnace."* Now that is what I call having FAITH.

The king got mad and commanded that these men be thrown into the furnace, which had been heated seven times more than the normal temperature. These men bowed down and worshipped God in the midst of their circumstance. God had already worked it out. When the king asked, "Did not we cast three men into the midst of the fire?" And then, "Why is it four men loose, walking in the midst of the fire, and they have no hurt, and the form of the fourth is like the Son of God?"

These mighty men came out of the furnace just like they had never gone in... I am going to stop and say, "Hallelujah!"Shadrach, Meshach, and Abednego's faith immediately got God's attention when they said, "Our God...is able to deliver..." They had full confidence and trust that God would "show up and show out," and He did. God wants us to always trust Him and know that He will move in our lives like He did in the lives of these men.

I am also reminded of another profound faith story mentioned in the Bible of the woman who had the issue of blood. You may have heard your Pastor speak of this story many times. This woman had experienced a deficiency in her blood. She had gone to several physicians, hoping to receive healing. I am certain she probably reached out to so many people, but heard criticism, gossip, etc. But, one day she learned that Jesus was going to be in town. She probably said, "I have gone through enough; I am tired; I have tried everything imaginable. My faith is going to get my Lord's attention today; I need to be healed."

This woman was so eager and had a made up mind that she was going to press her way through all kinds of people (judgmental, evil, angry, bitter...) to touch the hem of Jesus' garment. Upon one touch, she was healed. This kind of touch was so strong it pulled the virtue {strength, power} out of Jesus. Afterwards, He asked, "Who touched my clothes?" As the woman trembled, Jesus looked at her and told her to go in peace because her FAITH had made her whole (Mark, Chapter 5).The magnitude of the power behind this act of faith makes me want to touch the hem of Jesus' garment over and over again.

HAVE COURAGE

Each of us can stand to use the type of courage the woman with the issue of blood had. To have courage simply means to "be brave."We are in a season that requires us to be brave soldiers; we need to be radical and determined to get to Jesus no matter what is in our way. We need to keep pressing our way to the house of the Lord to be around others who are serious about moving forward in the Kingdom. God wants us to come to Him. We can no longer be concerned about the distractions, stumbling blocks, stone throwers, or anything else that is standing in our way. We have to navigate our way through these things.

Remember, "There is nothing too hard for our God." Some of you might yield to the spirit of worrying when things are not going as you would like for them to go. When this happens, many of you move from having faith to fear. You might find yourself saying, "If it isn't one thing, it's another." "I just don't know what to do." "This is too much for me." "I'm just going to quit." All kinds of unproductive words come out of your mouth when you are having thoughts of giving up.

But you cannot concentrate on the negative things that surround you; think about what is good, uplifting and positive. When you think on these things you will find yourself giving God thanks for what He has already done in your life, and you will have the strength and courage to depend on Him through your current situation. Nothing will be able to block what God has for you, and what He wants to do in your life.

HAVE PATIENCE

There will be times in life when we are going to be forced to just stand still, even in the "midst of our trials." Some people want the trials and tribulations they face to be reversed. If you are a person who needs to practice patience while going through...I said, "Going Through" the trials and tribulations, you can meditate on Romans 5:3 which says, "*...but we glory in tribulations also: knowing that tribulation* *worketh patience.* It is not the end for us when we go through trials and tribulations.

Many of us want to see immediate changes and results. I am here to tell you that everything does not always happen when we want it to happen, and everything does not disappear when we want it to disappear. Although sometimes there can be immediate results, there are other times it might just take a while. God has the perfect time for things to happen in each of our lives. "To everything there is a season..." (Ecclesiastes 3:1).You should stay focused on His promises. Do not get too in a hurry. If you lack patience, God will help you to become steadfast.

It is during these tough times that we need to be steadfast. If we focus too much on our problems and circumstances, we might become so desperate and move out of God's will. I am certain that you don't want to subject yourself to any other problems, so that is why there is a great need to practice patience in this life.

PERSERVERE

People of God, when you feel that you have come to a point to where you want to give up, I want to encourage you to keep going. You should keep pressing your way when "all odds are against you." And there will come a time in your life (if you haven't already experienced it) when you will feel like everyone and everything is against you. This is not uncommon at all.

We must learn how to persevere through every situation, even when it does not look so good, and is not pleasing to our eyes. Remember, everything is temporary, even life itself. There will be times in your life when expected and unexpected, good and bad things will happen. Those things that you have endured in life were present in that season to prepare you for a higher spiritual level. God had to see that you could endure that which seemed unbearable.

All the circumstances, rejection, criticism, and the mockery were there to point you in the direction of the Great I AM (God). This is always the right direction because all of us need to know that God is the One who will ultimately bring us out of any situation.

STAY FOCUSED ON GROWING

I believe that growth takes time, patience, commitment, focus and determination. You must have a desire to grow in every area of your life.

Once you focus on growing everything else will take its rightful place in your life. We are often put in certain situations that will compel us to grow. In some cases, "pain" can be associated with growth, too. I encourage you not to concentrate on the pain, but on your growth that is taking place. We may have to go through some things that might not feel so good, that includes being chastised (punished, whipped for being disobedient) by God, but it will be well worth it in the end. You will become a better person for the glory of God.

I have heard some people say, "God is not through with me yet; I am a work in progress." We all are a "work in progress."I can assure you that when God is done repairing you and filling you with the Holy Ghost, people will be able to see that you are a new person. When you have a mind to please God, you are opening your heart to growth.

So, are you ready to grow? Do you feel like you have already grown in most areas of your life? One way you can tell that you have grown is when you can immediately forgive someone who has offended you. I am certain you remember those times when someone offended you, and you wanted to retaliate by saying or doing something bad to them. Now you understand that God will fight every battle for you.

It also shows that you are sincere about growing when you no longer have a desire to do certain things in life, namely those things that you were a proud fan of doing. What I mean by this is that if you have been that person who likes to go to the club and party, or that person who likes to sleep around, or that person who always felt the need to lie about something, but you soon realized that none of these things pleased God, that is your assurance that you are heading in the right direction. God has given you a new desire—a desire to please Him and not your flesh. This is the best desire that any of us can have. The Word of God says, *"For they that are after the flesh do mind things of the flesh; but they that are after the Spirit do mind the things of the Spirit. For to be carnally minded is death; but to be spiritually minded is life and peace. Because the carnal mind is enmity (an enemy; have hatred) against God..."* (Romans 8:5-7).

DON'T STOP PRAYING

We need to make it our personal business to send a prayer to our Heavenly Father on a daily basis. Everything that we will (or have) ever face in life needs a touch of prayer. When we become too comfortable and stop praying, we will always be faced with something that will immediately send us back to the throne of God. We have to remember that our adversary is always looking for someone to annihilate (destroy, devour)—this is the devil's full-time job.

Do you remember those times you felt lonely and empty when you didn't pray? Do you remember feeling like the presence of God was not near during those times you stopped praying? Have you ever felt like you were just too weak to pray? Do you feel that you were being eaten alive by the devil's attacks during those times you were not in the prayer zone? If you have answered "Yes" to at least one of these questions, I'd like to encourage you to use your inner strength to "pray without ceasing." Prayer can and will make a big difference in your life.

INSPIRATION FOR YOUR HEART AND SOUL:
My sister, my brother, I decree and declare that everything that is standing in your way has to move. I want to encourage you to continue to walk in faith, have patience and keep the courage for you can overcome that fear and anxiety of what you are currently facing in life and what may come against you in the future.

PRAYER:

Lord, I thank you for increasing my faith in you. I thank you for allowing me to have the courage and the patience to wait on you. Because of you, I believe that I am able to endure in some of the most critical challenges of my life. I pray that you will continue to elevate me. I pray that you will bless me to grow in every area of my life. In Jesus name, Amen!

THOUGHT-PROVOKING QUESTIONS

Do you have faith? How would you rate your level of faith on a scale of 1-5?

1 is weak

2 is mild

3 is average

4 is above average

5 is strong

Has anything recently happened in your life to test your faith? If so, how was it tested? Would you say that you passed the test?

Do you have courage?

Do you lack patience? If so, what do you think it takes to help you have more patience?

Would you like to grow in every area of your life? What are the things that you believe is hindering your spiritual growth?

Do you only pray when things are not going right in your life? Do you only pray when you are seeking God for something that is going to benefit you? Do you only pray for yourself and your family?

CHAPTER 5
YOU ARE A CHILD OF GOD

"Whosoever believeth that Jesus is the Christ is born of God..."

(1 John)

Because you are...

CHRIST-LIKE

What did Jesus do while on earth? He healed the sick; He cast out devils; He fed the five thousand with two fish and five loaves, just to name a few. Jesus performed so many miracles, and before He was ascended to heaven He said, *"Verily, verily, I say unto you, He that believeth in me, the works that I do shall he do also; and greater works than these shall he do; because I go unto my Father"* (John 14:12).

Since Jesus told those of us who believe in Him that we would do greater works, we should have no problem executing everything He did. Each day we have a brand new opportunity to walk in love, feed the homeless, clothe the naked, encourage someone, pray for someone, lay hands on someone and decree and declare that they are made whole and so many other things by the power of God.

Oftentimes, we are put in situations whereby we are tested to see if we would do what Jesus did. Some people will fail the test the first time, but there are others who are always readily available and are led by God to reach out to people like Jesus did. When those opportunities are presented to us, we must ask ourselves, "What would Jesus do?" Some of you might ask, "What would you have me to do that would glorify you, Lord?" Either way, just ask Your Heavenly Father for guidance.

When we consult God about everything He will surely direct our path. Sometimes we can be moved by our emotions (and that could very well mean that we are in the flesh), but God will give us peace within our spirit when He has anything to do with our motives. We must make it all about Him, even when we are assisting others. It should never be about us. *"No flesh should ever glory in his presence"* (1 Corinthians 1:29).

I want to share an experience I had. One day I was enroute to work when my car stopped; my fuel pump went out. I had it towed to the shop and learned that it would cost a substantial amount of money to have it repaired. At the time I did not have enough funds to cover the cost of labor. I prayed about it and believed that God would supply my need. I immediately received a call from my co-worker after I said, "Amen." She said, *"God told me to call you to help you with the funds to get your car repaired, and I am going to be obedient."*

I was thankful for what God was doing through this lady. I went on to tell her how much money I had and what I needed. She told me that she would deposit it into my bank account. A few days later I learned that my car would need additional repairs which required more funds. Some church members were there to assist me. My car was repaired and I was ready to get back to driving. A week later I wrote my co-worker a check to repay her for the money she had helped me with. She gave it back to me and said, *"That was your gift; God told me to give it to you."* I give God all the glory. This was all about Him. This woman (and my church members) truly had the mind of Christ. Each of us should desire having this kind of mindset. We must be obedient to Him at all times.

I had another experience years ago. I had just arrived home from attending graduate school one Saturday when God told me to go to my sister's house to pray and lay hands on her. My sister had been sick for weeks. She had strep throat. I do not ever recall her being sick that long. She had gone to the doctor, but the medication that was prescribed was ineffective. I was mentally and physically tired from being in class for two days and having to travel back home (I live in Birmingham, Alabama but traveled from Montgomery where my classes were held), but I had to deny my flesh.

After God spoke to me, I immediately put my luggage down, went back out the door, got in my car and headed to my sister's house. When I arrived I went to her bedroom and stood on the side of the bed and laid my hands on her head. I told her husband to place his hands on her feet. I anointed her body with oil. We both began to pray. I prayed in the Spirit (an unknown tongue). I was reminded of what the Word says, "...*That if two of you shall agree on earth as touching anything that they shall ask, it shall be done for them of my Father which is in heaven*" (Matthew 18:19).

The Holy Ghost was moving in a mighty way while we were praying. God answered our prayers. My sister was healed on that day. She started speaking, after not being able to speak for days. She shared that she was in pain and that she had heard the voice of demons speaking (and a dark cloud had come over her) the night before in the spot where I was standing on the side of her bed. She explained that this had appeared to be a near death experience because she could barely breathe. As you can see, no matter what the devil tried to do to my sister, God intervened. When we are obedient to God and have faith in Him, we can perform these miracles just as Jesus did.

FIT FOR THE KINGDOM OF GOD

As believers of Jesus Christ, we are part of the kingdom of God. So, you are definitely a right fit for the Kingdom. Do not let anyone tell you differently. Just because your life may be a little rocky right now, it does not mean that you are unfit for the Kingdom of God. I want to encourage you to continue to set your heart and mind on doing Kingdom work, and God will continue to elevate you for His glory. You are on the right track. All you have to do is, "walk it out."

His word says, *"But seek ye first the kingdom of God, and his righteousness, and all these things shall be added unto you"* (Matthew 6:33).Therefore, we will suffer no lack. People of God we can have it all. An abundance of His blessings belongs to us because we are His beloved sons and daughters.

IN RIGHT STANDING WITH GOD

If you are thinking, "Am I not in right standing with God if I fall short of His glory? The answer is, "No". Although some people will condemn you to the pit of hell if you fall short of God's glory, you must remember that Jesus was not sent to condemn any of us. (John 3:17). Do not ever become too concerned about what people say. People are going to forever point out your faults (any little thing), especially people who are "holier than thou." You might be in the flesh every now and again. We all will get in the flesh sometimes. None of us will be in the spirit 24 hours a day, 7 days a week, or 365 days a year.

One thing to remember is that, "...*A just man falleth seven times, and riseth up again...*" (Proverbs 24:17). The key to this scripture is "riseth up again." You can never stay in that place of guilt and shame, and continue tormenting yourself. And do not let anyone else torment you. I am certain that when any of us get out of line with God, we can feel dirty and unworthy, but we have to come out of this place because there is a brighter side.

Each of us will make mistakes in life, but He convicts us so that we can immediately get back in line, and He chastises us because He loves us. He quickens (revive) our spirit when we are considering doing wrong because He wants us to repent and proceed to the way of truth and life. His grace and mercy will forever be sufficient and it will follow us throughout our life's journey.

A ROYAL PRIESTHOOD

The Bible says that we are "a royal priesthood, a holy nation, and a peculiar people." God has called each of us out of darkness, and you have stepped into His marvelous light. He has made us to be that light in those very dark places. The light of Jesus that is within us should be shining in our homes and everywhere else we go.

We believers live in this sinful world, but we should not participate in the worldly acts that are contrary to God's Word. People of God we must practice doing that which is pleasing to Him. *"For thou art an holy people unto the Lord thy God: the Lord thy God hath chosen thee to be a special people unto himself, above all people that are upon the face of the earth"* (Deuteronomy 7:6).

We are peculiar, meaning that our character should resemble God's character. The people of the world should be able to see the essence of God in our lives. They should desire to be like us in that respect, because we are following God. When He is at the helm of our lives, we will always end up in the right place.

INSPIRATION FOR YOUR HEART AND SOUL:

My sister, my brother, God knows that you have a strong desire to please Him daily. No matter what obstacles come in your direction, continue to exemplify godly character. "You are a servant of righteousness."

PRAYER:

Lord, I thank you for seeing a reflection of your Son, Jesus on the inside of me. I thank you for allowing me to be transparent so that the lost souls can also see you on the inside of me so they may be drawn nigh unto you. I pray that you will continue blessing me to walk in integrity and in love. In Jesus name, Amen!

THOUGHT-PROVOKING QUESTIONS

Would you say that you are a child of God? Would you like to experience the mindset that Jesus had according to Philippians 2:5? Based on your lifestyle, do you feel as though you already possess the mindset that Jesus had according to that scripture?

Do you believe that you are fit for the kingdom of God? Has anyone ever told you that you are not fit for the kingdom of God? Can you even imagine how the kingdom of God is?

Do you believe that you are walking upright before God? What do you believe that God would say about your present lifestyle?

Would you say that your character resembles the character of God? What are some attributes you have that Jesus would probably be proud of?

CHAPTER 6
YOU ARE PURPOSED

All things work together...them who are called according to his {God} purpose."

(Romans 8:28)

To...

WORSHIP GOD ALMIGHTY

Worshipping God is so important, and it is something each of us truthfully owes Him. We should always worship God, whether we are young or old. As a matter of fact, "We were created to worship God."The Bible says, *"And it shall come to pass, that from one new moon to another, and from one Sabbath to another, shall all flesh come to worship before me, saith the Lord"* (Isaiah 66:23). When we worship God, we are inviting Him to come into our home, our job, or wherever we are. Likewise, we are entering into His presence. But, we have to be real and true worshippers. *"They that worship Him must worship Him in spirit and in truth"* (John 4:24).

God is a Spirit. Therefore, we cannot worship God in the flesh, or put any trust and confidence in it. Our flesh does not need to be acknowledged when we come into the presence of our Heavenly Father. We will always fail when we try to worship God in the flesh. A prime example of what I mean by this is that if you are in attendance at a church service or an event where there is a time of praise and worship, and you are focusing on how someone else is praising and worshipping God, and you try to emulate what that person is doing, then there is a strong indication that you are in the flesh. God is definitely not honored by this act of worship. It is not real.

This kind of fleshly act of worshipping God is so common in settings such as churches, conferences and similar events. Many people yield their flesh and not their spirit. You cannot focus on other people, places or things. When you focus on what someone else is doing, it will always take your focus off God. He should always be our main focus. We should offer God all that we have within us. The atmosphere needs to be as peaceful as possible, and our mind has to be free of fear, anxiety, anger, stress, worry, or anything else that will hinder us from being totally in God's presence.

Each of us may have a different worship experience with God. As long as it is sincere and from within your spirit, God honors and receives it. I have personally heard God speak to me while in the midst of worship. Some people may experience instant healing, while others may experience a breakthrough that they have been praying for. Some of the things that God does while you are worshipping Him will blow your mind. It will even make you start "praising Him in advance" for what He is in the process of doing.

PRAISE GOD UNLIMITED

We have every reason every day to praise our Heavenly Father. Psalm 150:6 says, *"Let everything that hath breath praise the Lord. Praise ye the Lord."* That scripture should penetrate your heart and move you in the direction of praise. Whether we are going to give God praise should never be contingent upon how we feel. It does not matter how we feel. A sacrifice has to be made. If you are too tired, just "shake it off" and talk to the One who can give you strength.

If you just take a moment to think about all the hurtful and bad things you have endured and how far you have come, you should boldly say, *"His praise shall continually be in my mouth"* (Psalm 34:1). You might even be experiencing something that is not so good right now. Your children could be acting up. Your enemies could be plotting against you. Your finances may be low. You could be facing layoff on your job. Trouble could just be coming from every direction. But wait—you can start "praising your way out" of your situation.

You can make the following declarations to the Lord:

- I believe that if I praise you Lord, you are going to make my enemies act right.
- I believe that if I praise you Lord, you are going to give me favor with all mankind.
- I believe that if I praise you Lord, you are going to make my husband get in line.
- I believe that if I praise you Lord, you are going to make my wife get in line.
- I believe that if I praise you Lord, you are going to make my children get in line.
- I believe that if I praise you Lord, you are going to heal my body.
- I believe that if I praise you Lord, you are going to give me a spiritual promotion.
- I believe that if I praise you Lord, you are going to pour out financial blessings upon me.

- I believe that if I praise you Lord, you are going to bless me with the job that I have been praying for.
- I believe that if I praise you Lord, you are going to increase my ministry.

When we praise God, it opens the door of expectancy. We can expect the blessings of God to flow into our lives from Heaven. I am certain you like receiving the blessings of God.

BE THE HEAD AND NOT THE TAIL

"You are the head and not the tail; above and not beneath." Now is the time for you to come to the front of the line, and to be on top of things for the glory of God. You have become so familiar withbeing at the bottom of the barrel. It can no longer be your safe haven. God has more for you, my sister and my brother.

You have been in the same situation way too long. It has had a tight grip on your life, and it has gotten the best of you. The lack that you have suffered in many areas of your life has kept you in bondage. It has placed you in a position to constantly ask people for some sort of help. Your problems and circumstances have been in charge. It is time for you to be in charge. It is time for you to succeed, to prosper, to speak life, and to go higher. I want to stop right now and say a pray for you.

God, I come before your throne of grace on behalf of your people who have been in lack and I ask you to increase them in every area of their life. They have been cheerful givers, Lord. You told us to "Give and it shall be given unto you; good measure, pressed down, and shaken together, and running over, shall men give into your bosom..." (Luke 6:38). We trust everything you said in Your Word, Lord, and we know that it cannot be returned void unto you. You spoke it God and it has to manifest in our lives. Give us favor with men and women, and most of all You! We thank you in advance God for not only hearing our prayers, but answering them. We will have hearts of expectancy, and like Jacob (who wrestled with one of your Angels), we won't let you go until you bless us. (Read Genesis 32:24-26). In Jesus name, Amen!

God will give you the power to surpass your problems and circumstances. You have to change your way of thinking. You must also learn to be a wise steward over what God has already given you. Stop "settling for less." Decree and declare that you are the "lender and not the borrower,""the head and not the tail," strong and not weak, rich and not poor, whole and not broken, free and not bound. The Bible says, *"The thief cometh not but for to steal, and to kill, and to destroy: I am come that they might have life, and that they might have it more abundantly"* (John 10:10). Although our adversary wants to take from us, God wants each of us to experience an abundant life. Let us examine our lives daily, and make sure that we are in the right position to receive what God has for us.

FULFILL WHAT GOD HAS CALLED YOU TO DO

We as believers were sought out by God before our birth to fulfill what He has called each of us to do. Some of us may have similar assignments, but the key is seeking God on what He has specifically called you to do. You do not need to be concerned with what your pastor, your mother, your father, your friend, your co-worker or anyone else is doing. The call upon your life is only between you and God.

When I was studying the book of Exodus, I learned that Moses was called by God to deliver the children of Israel out of Egypt. When God called Moses to do this task, no one else was there but Moses and the angel of the Lord that appeared unto him in a flame of fire out of the midst of a bush (Exodus 3:2). Moses did not think that he was qualified to execute something of that magnitude which God had instructed him to do because of his speaking ability. Seemingly, Moses dealt with the fear of speaking before people. Besides, he did not think that the children of Israel would listen to him.

Moses told the Lord, *"O my Lord, I am not eloquent, neither heretofore, nor since thou hast spoken unto thy servant: but I am slow of speech, and of a slow tongue. And the Lord said unto him, who hath made man's mouth? Or who maketh the dumb, or deaf, or the seeing, or the blind? Have not I the Lord? Now therefore go, and I will be with thy mouth, and teach thee what thou shalt say"* (Exodus 4:10-12).

In Exodus 4:16, God told Moses that he would use his brother Aaron to be his spokesman. But the more God spoke to Moses concerning addressing the children of Israel, the more confident Moses became with his assignment to deliver those who were in bondage. Some of you may see yourself the same way Moses saw himself. The devil has told you that you are not qualified; you do not have the credentials; you do not have a PhD; you have never spoken before people, so you will not do well; people are not going to receive you; they do not want to hear what you have to say. But, what did God say about you? That is all that matters. You do not have to accept anything negative from people.

If it does not line up with what the Lord said, then you should turn a deaf ear to it. You do not have to listen to the lies the devil has told you. Remember, Satan will use anyone to speak against your calling, even some of our spiritual leaders. One thing to remember is that the call upon your life is all about God. You must trust that God will guide you through what He has chosen you to do just as He guided Moses through what He anointed and appointed him to do.

When your focus is solely on pleasing Almighty God, then you will find that inner peace to carry out the mission at hand. Your confidence will greatly increase because you know that God is on your side. Your purpose in life will always be far greater than what people say and what people do. One writer said, "Passion produces purposes." With that being said, just think back to what you have always enjoyed doing, even as an innocent child. Whatever you had so much fun doing may very well be associated with what God has called you do while here on earth.

INSPIRATION FOR YOUR HEART AND SOUL:

My sister, my brother, each of us has a purpose that God wants us to fulfill. I encourage you to seek God about your purpose. He will reveal it to you. Just because you have not gotten it all together, does not mean that you do not have a purpose. You might have been in the back of the line, but God is going to move you the front of the line.

PRAYER:

Lord, I am so thankful that I am able to worship and praise you. I pray that you will continue to move in my life and bless me to do what it is that you have called me to do. Lord, give me the strength and confidence to carry out my mission. In Jesus name, Amen!

THOUGHT-PROVOKING QUESTIONS

Do you like worshipping God? Do you need to hear worship music in order to yield your mind, body, and spirit to Him in your car, home, church, etc?

Do you believe that you should praise God daily? If so, do you now praise Him daily for what He has done in your life? Do you praise Him for what He has done in the lives of others?

Do you believe that you are the head and not the tail?

Do you really want to fulfill your purpose in life? Do you know what your purpose is in life? If so, would you say that you have truly been walking in your purpose? If not, have you been seeking God about it? Are you depending on your pastor or minister to reveal your purpose to you?

CHAPTER 7
YOU ARE ANOINTED

"The Spirit of the Lord is upon me; because the Lord hath anointed me to..."

(Isaiah 61:1)

To...

BE A GREAT LEADER

"**When** the righteous are in authority, the people rejoice: but when the wicked beareth rule, the people mourn" (Proverbs 29:2). Think about this: Jesus was a leader, and the people who believed in Jesus while He was here on earth rejoiced as they followed Him. They believed that Jesus would lead them in the right direction. All believers should feel this way. Being a righteous leader is not limited to the clergy {religious officials}, such as ministers, pastors, apostles, evangelist, and bishops. It also includes those who are in leadership positions on your job, and even in your home. If the leader is righteous, then the people will no doubt rejoice. And people do not mind following these types of leaders. If your leader is wicked, God will remove you from under that kind of leadership in

His timing. "Just stand still and know that He is God."

When a person has the mind of Christ and is submitted to Him, they can become a great leader because everything about Jesus Christ is great. If you are anointed to lead, you can go ahead and wear the anointing with full confidence; knowing that Jesus will direct your path. If you are new at leading, make sure you stay connected to great leaders, especially your spiritual leaders. The anointing of God that is on their life will trickle down and positively affect those who are following. These men and women of God have been chosen to lead. The Word of God says, "...I will give you pastors according to mine heart, which shall feed you with knowledge and understanding" (Jeremiah 3:15).

There are a vast number of pastors (and other spiritual leaders) who are sincere about helping to nurture new and emerging leaders. True growth can take place when someone is properly nurtured. These pastors do not just want to pour into the lives of the up and coming leaders; they want to see the whole body of Christ grow. These pastors have a heart of God, and they are submitted to God. With that being said, it is an act of our obedience to God to submit to their authority.

God has allowed them to see your potential so that they can help you in the area of leading. Believe me! Many of them have crossed some bridges that some of the new leaders must cross on their journey. I am certain those leaders who are sold out to Jesus Christ have to deal with our adversary when he throws his best fiery darts at them. For example, when that devil is using some of those who say they will walk with the leader, yet they slander their name. When the leader is on the battlefield, they fight against them instead of fighting with them. When they see their leader get in the flesh (this happens to all of us at times), they condemn them to hell. Let me say this: If you see a flaw in the man or woman of God, do not judge them; instead, pray and lift them up before God.

I remember those times when I passed judgment on some of our spiritual leaders. We must leave the judgment of anyone up to Our Heavenly Father—the only One who sits in the mercy seat. I had to ask God to forgive me. I now pray more and more for each of our spiritual leaders, and other leaders as well. God is moving me in the direction of leadership, and I want everything He has for me. I do not want anything to hinder my blessings. I have learned that obedience is the key, and being humble in the process will open many doors for me. I am truly honored to submit to my pastor's leadership. He is well seasoned and has a heart for God's people.

I encourage any new leaders to submit to the spiritual leader that God has placed over you. I am certain you have heard something to this effect: "One must be a good follower in order to be a good leader." Do not assume that you are not under the leadership that God wants you to be, or do not get sidetracked by the negative things that people are speaking against your leader. If you personally feel a negative way toward the man or woman of God, just go to God in prayer.

As you continue in prayer, and continue to grow, God will give you clear instructions on what to do next. If God wants to place you under a new leader for what He has purposed you to do, He will make sure you depart from your local church with proper notice and integrity. If God is ready to release you in that leading role, He still wants you to do things in order. I realize the importance of doing things in order with respect to letting your leader know what God has placed on your heart, because those who truly have the heart of God will give their blessings to you, and pray for your ministry, too.

SPEAK WITH CONFIDENCE

By the grace God, each of us has something that we are very good at doing. Some people are anointed to sing. I love listening to Marvin Sapp, Shirley Ceasar, Yolanda Adams, CeCe Winans, and so many others who sing songs of praise and worship. These great singers have beautiful voices, and they are all using their voices to the glory of God. Some people are anointed to cook. I have eaten certain people's cooking and the taste of the food had me coming back for more. Some people are anointed to write articles, books, etc. These people have a special way of inspiring people through their written words. T.D. Jakes is one of my favorite authors.

When God has anointed you to lead people, you will be able to boldly proclaim the Word of God. When you first start speaking before people, you might feel a little shaky, but as times progresses, you will have the confidence to speak to the multitude without an ounce of fear or nervousness. The anointing of God will strengthen you, and He will speak through you. God will always give you a Word that will convict, build, heal and deliver His people. Some people will be drawn closer to God, because of how you (or someone you know who is anointed to speak) convey the message of hope, healing and deliverance to those who are hurting, in bondage, or those who are seeking God about something else.

God has helped me over the years to become stronger when speaking before people. I remember when I was very shy and did not feel confident at one point. My words did not always come out as clear as I would have liked for them to. But I had to trust that God would put His Words in my mouth. The more I began to lean on Him as I stood before people, and denied my flesh, the more comfortable and confident I became. I must admit, from time to time I still get a little shaky, but I am always reminded of the vision that God gave me back in 2007. He told me, "Now go and carry the mantle." I saw myself speaking before the masses. I have to continue to trust what He told me and showed me, and believe that people will be blessed by what He speaks through me.

I want to encourage someone who is reading this book, who may have tried to make excuses about how they speak, or have just had the fear of speaking before people, to trust God. Rewind back to what He showed you, and told you years ago. Remember, God will put His Words in your mouth just like He told Moses He would do for Him. He has anointed you to share His Word with the people, so you have to do it His way. When you make it all about God, and get out of your flesh, you will excel as a great speaker. Doing public speaking may not be your area, so it may take a little time if you are new at this, but the more you speak before people, the more comfortable you will become. Your words will be more powerful, stronger, and clearer for the glory of God.

SERVE OTHERS WITH THE HEART OF GOD

God is well pleased with us when we have a heart to serve others. The Bible says, *"But he that is greatest among you shall be your servant"* (Matthew 23:11).There are many servants of God who are laboring daily, denying their flesh, and committing their spirit to prayer and fasting, for the lost souls in the world to accept Jesus Christ and submit to His will.

It is the will of our Heavenly Father that we as believers serve. We must always be mindful that there are a vast number of hurting people who exist in this "dying world." Many of them are in bondage, crying out to God like the children of Israel did. And God is calling upon His servants to reach out to these people.

Our hearts have to be pure in order for us to willfully serve others. There can be no signs of selfishness. We must be compassionate enough to think of other people. Real servants are always in a "ready mode" to hear God's voice on what to do next. Even more, these people yield every part of their being to go above and beyond to bless others. They will put a 100% trust in God, knowing that He will always have their back.

BREAK THE GENERATIONAL CURSES

Many families have generations of alcoholics, adulterers, gamblers, drug abusers, murderers, liars, and the list goes on. These are generational curses that can be broken by the power of God. It is not a coincidence that you are the one who has been called the castaway among your family members. Yet, God has chosen you to help break the curses in your family. People have looked down on you, but while they were looking down, you were looking up to your only source—God. You may have found yourself succumbing to one of the sins mentioned above that had a stronghold on your family for generations, but God has allowed you to clearly recognize the curse that is in your family's blood line.

Although you were a victim of one of these sins, God has delivered you, and He has anointed you; that is why you have been able to go through the storms and come out of them with a stronger level of faith and discernment. The anointing that is on your life will help destroy the yokes of bondage in your family. You are in the right position to help your family because you have submitted to God. You believe in the power of the Holy Ghost, and you know that God called you out of darkness so that you can help your family.

Do not fear! You are already equipped to make a difference in your family. You know the importance of speaking life into their lives at all times, showing unconditional love, believing they can be free from anything that has been hindering their growth. I am in agreement with you and decree and declare that whatever strongholds have gripped your family will not continue to go from generation to generation. It will be broken in the name of Jesus Christ.

INSPIRATION FOR YOUR HEART AND SOUL:
My sister, my brother, God has placed a special anointing on some of our lives. I encourage you to use the anointing to the glory of God. The anointing will help you to lead and speak with confidence. It will

also destroy the yokes of division, abuse, addiction, and many other curses in your family.

PRAYER:

Lord, I thank you for anointing me. I thank you for purging all of the things that are not like you from within me. I thank you for giving me a servant's heart. I pray that you will continue to use me to bring my family together, and to be a blessing to your people. In Jesus name, Amen!

THOUGHT-PROVOKING QUESTIONS

Do you know any great leaders? Are you a leader, or an emerging leader? If so, do you use your leadership position to control others? Would you say that people like following you?

Are you afraid to speak in front of others? Do you believe that you have the ability to speak with confidence?

Do you enjoy serving others with the heart of God? If so, what kinds of things have you recently done to serve others?

Do you believe that you have the power through Jesus Christ to break the generational curses in your family? What are some of the curses that are plaguing your family?

CHAPTER 8
YOU HAVE BEEN RECONCILED TO GOD

"And all things are God, who hath reconciled us to himself by Jesus Christ, and hath given to us the ministry of reconciliation"
(2 Corinthians 5:19).

You have...

THE BLOOD OF JESUS COVERING YOU

In the book of Exodus, Chapter 12, God had instructed Moses and Aaron to speak to the congregation of Israel so that they could prepare the way for what was called, The Lord's Passover. During the Passover, God brought judgment on the Egyptians. God wanted to protect the children of Israel from destruction so they were instructed to take a lamb that was without blemish (a flaw), and they had a certain length of time to keep the lamb before they had to kill it. They were then instructed to put the blood of the lamb on the two side door posts and on the upper door post of the house. In verse 18, the Lord spoke saying, "...the blood shall be to you for a token upon the houses where ye are:

and when I see the blood, I will pass over you, and the plague shall not be upon you to destroy you, when I smite the land of Egypt."

While the lamb was an animal that was sacrificed during the time of the Passover, the blood of the lamb was a way for the Lord to identify the houses that the children of Israel occupied. But now we have the blood of Jesus which covers us believers. He is the Lamb of God. God sent Jesus to sacrifice His life, and this is how we have been reconciled back to Him. The blood that Jesus shed has so much power; that "blood never loses its power." It is a strong protection for us. I am so grateful for the blood of Jesus covering us, even when some of us do wrong. Each of us has done wrong at some point in our lives. The good thing is that Jesus still sees a reflection of Himself in those of us who believe in Him.

I can truly testify about how Jesus' blood has continually protected my family. One night I dreamed of blood raining from the sky. I ran outside to put my arms around this baby that was sitting alone. I began to pray for this baby and while in the midst of prayer, I held my head up when the voice of a lady came from a different direction, saying, "Stop praying in the spirit like that." I continued to pray, and then woke up out of my dream. I asked God to reveal to me what that dream was all about.

He later revealed it to me one Saturday morning through one of the ministers at my former church prior to having prayer intercession. On that morning some of the ladies at the church gathered and we talked about various things, from how God delivered us to where He has brought us on our journey. I shared with them the dream I had and how I had been seeking God about it. The minister told me that God had revealed to her that I was covering my first born. She encouraged me to continue to pray for my child.

It was nearly a week later when I got a call that my child had driven two co-workers home from work around 2:00 a.m. and was stopped by the police in the parking lot of where one of the co-workers lived. My child did not have her driver's license at the time of this incident, and she was driving one of my sibling's vehicles who she was living with. When the policeman came to the car he detected the scent of marijuana. After he did his normal routine, each of them was free to go. The car was not towed and neither one of them went to jail. My sibling was contacted to come and pick up my child.

If you are thinking, *"Is that it?"* Yes, that is it because God blocked the handiwork of the enemy. It was the power in the blood of Jesus and His awesome grace and mercy that covered my child. Jesus protects all of us in the same manner. Let me say this: We must continue to pray for our children and those who might not have a consistent prayer life. Your unselfish prayers can help someone else. *"...The effectual fervent prayer of a righteous man availeth much"* (James 5:16).

I am certain many of you reading this book can remember when your back was up against the wall. You were doing something you had no business doing. The same blood that covered my child on the night of incident is the same blood that covered me when I was not doing the will of God, and it is the same blood that covered you, too.

THE FAVOR OF GOD ON YOUR LIFE

The favor of God is one great reward. It is an extension of God's love toward us. I have heard people say, "Favor is not fair." I would like to say that "favor is fair." To have the favor of God on your life is to be blessed beyond measure by Him. Many of us can testify about the goodness of God and how

He has given us a special kind of favor, even when we did not think we deserved it.

God's favor comes with many advantages. Some of you may have already experienced some of these favors that I am about to mention:

- It was the favor of God upon your life when you remained in your position and several of your co-workers were recently laid off due to downsizing of the company.
- It was the favor of God upon your life when you were hired by a company that required extensive years of experience, but you had no experience in this line of work.
- It was the favor of God upon your life when your apartment manager offered you a two-month-free rent move-in special when all the other new tenants only received one month free rent.
- It was the favor of God upon your life when you went to pay a utility bill and learned that it was already paid.
- It was the favor of God upon your life when you paid less for the best; that includes cars, clothes, furniture, etc.

- It was the favor of God upon your life when that stranger walked up to you and said, "God told me to give this money to you."

The favor of God goes way beyond our imagination. We will never be able to fathom (comprehend) the mind of God. He works in "mysterious" ways. He does whatever He wants to do at any given time. There are so many other favor advantages that many believers are experiencing on a daily basis.

A HOLY WEAPON TO FIGHT THE ADVERSARY'S ATTACKS

We all have 24 hour access to the same weapon which is the Holy Bible—the Word of God. It will help renew your mind, comfort your hurting heart, increase your faith, and erase your fears. It will also give you peace, give you hope, give you strength, and so much more.

This weapon can help us to combat all of Satan's attacks. These attacks can come in any form {financial, emotional, and mental distress, sickness, etc). Although these attacks are meant to harm us, there is a written scripture in the Bible for every one of them.

Jesus experienced many attacks while here on earth, and He fought against them with the Word of God. When He was led by the spirit into the wilderness, and tempted by Satan while on a forty day fast, He simply told Satan, "It is written..."(Read Luke 4:1-8). After you read these scriptures, you should find the confidence in knowing that you can handle every attack through the Word of God.

THE VICTORY

We have the victory through our Lord Jesus Christ (1 Corinthians 15:57). We are in a race everyday. There is no need for any of us to focus on the rate of our speed or someone else's speed; we just need to keep running for our reward is great. The Bible says, "...let us run with patience..." (Hebrews 12:2).

The tempter (Satan, our adversary) is going to try to take you off track. He is going to throw his fiery darts. He is going to tell you that you are a loser. He is going to tell you that you are not worthy of God's best. He is going to tell you that no one loves you. He is going to tell you that you cannot go any further. He is going to tell you that you are not smart enough to go to school. He is going to tell you that you cannot be healed. He is going to tell you that he has a better offer if you serve him. He is going to tell you all manner of foolishness.

Remember, everything that Satan tells you is intended to make you quit on God. I want to tell you that Satan has been speaking all of his lies to you to try to make you quit—do not quit. Stand firm on the Word of God. You have come too far to turn back and start all over. You can go ahead and claim your victory.

Whenever Satan throws something in your direction, you throw it back at him even harder! You do not ever have to be afraid because God is always surrounding you. While Satan is speaking lies to you, you began to speak life. You tell him that you are winner; that you are worthy of God's best; that God loves you more than anything; that you will make it to the finish line; that you have the wisdom of God to do anything you set your mind to do; that you are healed in the name of Jesus.

STRENGTH

I was sitting at my computer one day, and a spirit of depression came over me. I had a choice to entertain it and let it steal my joy, or speak with authority, commanding it to leave. Well,I immediately began to use the power that God bestowed upon me, and spoke the Word of God ("the joy of the Lord is my strength") to cast out that spirit of depression. If you are thinking, "How can I use my inner strength to cast out a spirit?" It goes back to what I shared earlier; you must speak the Word of God ("it is written...") to whatever that situation is.

Remember, the Word of God is more powerful than anything else on earth. In essence, it is our strength. Each of us has the inner strength that He has freely given to us, and we must always use it to overcome certain things that come up against us on a daily basis. There is no need for us to become dismayed or distressed—"we have the power" through the power of Christ Jesus!

INSPIRATION FOR YOUR HEART AND SOUL:

My sister, my brother, you can rest assure that "you are in the right hands"—you are in God's hand. Jesus made this connection for us. When you said, "I believe," you said enough. I encourage you to stay in the will of Your Heavenly Father for your greatest reward is eternal life.

PRAYER:

Lord, I thank you for placing a shield of protection around me. I thank you for giving me favor with you and with mankind. I pray that you will give me the strength to stay in the race, and a mindset to finish whatever I start. In Jesus name, Amen!

THOUGHT-PROVOKING QUESTIONS

Do you believe that there is power in the blood that Jesus shed on Calvary?

Would you say that you have the favor of God on your life? If so, what are some experiences that led you to believe that you have the favor of God on your life? If not, would you like to experience the favor of God? Do you think that you can earn the favor of God by being obedient? What about helping others?

Are you using the Bible as your weapon against Satan's attacks? If not, what weapon are you using? If so, can you share some of those experiences and how God's Word has helped you to combat those attacks?

What are some things that you have the victory over? Do you encourage others to stay in the victory race?

Do you really believe that you have inner strength? How are you using your inner strength to overcome certain things in your life?

CHAPTER 9
YOU CAN REJOICE IN THE LORD

"Rejoice in the Lord, O ye righteous..."
(Psalm 33:1)

For it is God who...

DELIVERED YOU

It was God who delivered each of us from out of bondage. We have all been bound by something. God has brought us so far on our journey. From victim to virtuous, from poverty to plenty, from bitterness to gladness, from bondage to freedom, from brokenness to wholeness, from pain to joy, from ill to heal, from rejection to relationship with God. From where God has brought us, it is enough to say, "Hallelujah!"

I had been in several bad relationships fornicating. I felt that there was no way out. I am very thankful for God delivering me. As I reflect upon my deliverance, I am reminded that there are people all across the globe that are still in bondage. Some people are bound by adultery, drugs, gambling, and so many other things. These people do not have to stay in that place of fear, confusion and discomfort. The Bible says, *"The Spirit of the*

Lord is upon me (Jesus), because he hath anointed me to preach the gospel to the poor; he hath sent me to heal the brokenhearted, to preach deliverance to the captives, and recovering of sight to the blind, to set at liberty them that are bruised" (Luke 4:18).

If you find yourself in some sort of situation that seems inescapable, this scripture should give you comfort in knowing that if you have a desire to come out of bondage, Jesus can help you. God does not want us to live in bondage. He is honored to bring us out of those situations that plague our lives. Once God delivers us, He wants us to move forward and experience freedom and an abundance of His blessings.

HEALED YOU

God is able to heal every part of our life (physically, emotionally, spiritually, etc), with His miracle working power. The Word of God says that we are healed with Jesus stripes. (Isaiah 53:5). If you were diagnosed with a disease {Aids, diabetes, cancer, lupus, etc}, and you no longer have it, it was God who healed you. Every disease that has been diagnosed was carried to the cross—Jesus bore them for us. When you have faith in God and consistently speak healing over yourself, your healing will soon manifest. Remember, life and death is in the power of your tongue. (Proverbs 18:21).

Some of you may have been emotionally sick, but God has healed your emotional wounds. God has given you the strength to release those things that you have been emotionally attached to—those things that have drained you, whether it was an unhealthy relationship, an abusive marriage, a bad friendship or a dead-end job. It could have very well been something else. Since you have been healed in this area of your life, it is important that you keep your emotions under control so that you will not repeat those life cycles that had you emotionally bound.

God has healed those of you who have had your spiritual struggles. What I mean by this is that you may have been hurt by another Christian. Perhaps someone who has been attending church services for many years. That might even include your pastor, your pastor's wife, your associate pastor, a deacon, a choir member, an usher, etc. Being hurt by another Christian is not uncommon; it happens frequently within the church body. The hurt that some of you may have faced from another Christian could have stemmed from gossip, betrayal, and infidelity for those of you who are married.

When people are hurt by these types of things that happen in the church, it not only affects the person who has been hurt, but the Christian body as a whole. Oftentimes people will leave a church because they have been impacted by those things that I mentioned. They might not feel the love of God (that we as Christians should execute) within the walls of the church. There are others who will not come to church because they hear and see what goes on in some churches. No matter what kind of hurt we experience, God is able to heal us.

GAVE YOU THE VISION

It was God who gave you a vision of your purpose, your business, your spouse, etc. The manifestation of that vision is very near, just stay focused. The Bible says, "...Write the vision, and make it plain upon tables, that he may run that readeth it: For the vision is yet for an appointed time, but at the end it shall speak, and not lie: though it tarry, wait for it; because it will surely come, it will not tarry (Habakkuk 2:2-3).

It was God who gave you a vision of your purpose; He will make sure you have everything you need to carry it out. There is no need to be in a hurry. You shall reign in His timing. You do not have to continue trying to get people to understand what God is doing in your life concerning your purpose. All you have to do is "stand still," trust God, obey, summit and commit to His will.

It was God who gave you a vision of that business you want to start. You can go ahead and invest time and money into your business, even though it has not come to fruition. Everything that you have envisioned it to be will be so. God is gathering your customers, so you do not have to beg those naysayers to support your business. He will also make sure you have people of integrity working with you.

It was God who showed you that you will get married. You may have had several bad relationship experiences, but this does not mean that you are not qualified for marriage. God has had to do some things in your life; He has taught you how to be a wife and a husband—people who understand the dynamics of marriage and its purpose, which is ministry. He has not ignored your prayers concerning marriage; just know that it will happen in His timing.

God will always give us a glimpse of what is about to take place in our lives. You must know that during the "waiting period" He is preparing you for what He has shown you. I remember when He gave me a vision of my purpose and my ministry back in 2007. I had a vision that I was speaking to a large group of women. All I could see were women as far as my eyes could behold. Later, God spoke to me about what my purpose would entail.

While He was speaking, He showed me a group of women in a jail cell. I saw myself running toward the cell with a key; I unlocked the door and the women exited. Their faces looked as if they were hurt, discouraged—broken. I learned that I was assigned to help broken girls and women navigate their way through brokenness. It has been manifested in my life. Although I have spoken at a few engagements, God has started opening doors for more speaking engagements. I truly thank God. The vision shall surely come to pass if we just believe and hold on to God's promises.

DESERVES ALL THE GLORY

It is very common to give someone accolades when they achieve in life. This is not wrong to do; however, we should look to the source (God) that made it possible. Oftentimes we look at other people as if they gave us the talents and made it possible for us to use those talents to do great things in our lives. We can never do anything without our

Heavenly Father. We should never forget that He works through people. With that being said, we should always be thankful and give Him glory.

He deserves all the praise, worship, honor, and glory for everything that He has already done in our lives, and for what He has in store for us. You should never get to a point where you think that you (or anyone else) should be glorified, because no one (I mean no one) can do bigger things than our God. And no one is better or greater than Him. No one deserves to receive the highest praise, but God. 1 Corinthians 10:31 says, "...whatsoever ye do, do all to the glory of God."

You should give God glory for planting those thoughts of success in your head, for transforming your life, for making you the head and not the tail, for giving you favor, for saving you and your child, for fighting your battle, for making you debt free, for giving you that promotion, for giving you wealth, for providing a place to live, for making you a leader, for bringing you out of bondage, for making your enemies treat you right, for giving you peace of mind in the midst of turbulent times, for blessing you with transportation, for blessing you with the knowledge to obtain your degree...I can go on sharing what God has done in our lives.

INSPIRATION FOR YOUR HEART AND SOUL:

My sister, my brother, you can rejoice in the Lord for all the awesome things He has done in your life. I want to encourage you to stay on a godly path, and make sure everything you do and say is to the Glory of God.

PRAYER:

Lord, I thank you for everything that you have done for me. I am so excited about the things that you have in store for me. I pray that you will keep your hands on my life. Lord, help me to be strong so that I can keep going forward and not think of going backward. Lord, I give only you the Glory. In Jesus name, Amen!

THOUGHT-PROVOKING QUESTIONS

Do you believe that you have truly been delivered from several things in your life? What are some of those things? Are you happy about being delivered from those things?

Are you now experience sickness? Were you told that there was no hope for your illness? Do you believe that you are healed according to Isaiah 53:5? Do you have affirmations about healing that you state daily?

Have you had a vision of starting your own business, writing a book, acting, etc? If so, was it very clear to you? Did you write the vision down? Do you feel comfortable sharing it with your family and friends? Do you believe that it will come to fruition?

Would you agree that God deserves all the glory? Have you ever given someone else the glory above God, including yourself?

CHAPTER 10
YOU ARE BLESSED

"...There shall be showers of blessings."
(Ezekiel 34:26)

So you can...

REAP A HARVEST FOR YOUR FAITHFULNESS

There are faithful laborers out in the field (at work, in the store, at church, etc) witnessing to the lost souls everyday. The song says, "For your faithfulness, it's your time." I have to agree with the words of this song. The Heavenly chart that God keeps on each of us shows the good and the bad that we have done up to this point of our lives. Your faithfulness, dedication, and diligence have been recorded by God. And He wants to reward you for the good seeds that you have sown.

My sister and my brother, God wants to give you everything that you have asked Him for. Your commitment to God has opened the door for so many things. His blessing will shower down on you in this season of your life. You will be filled with a new level of faith, a new level of anointing, a new level of patience, and a new level of peace...just trust God with all your heart. His promises shall be fulfilled in your life.

BECOME A GOOD STEWARD WITH YOUR BLESSINGS

It is very important that we practice being good stewards with our blessings. Whether it is a small blessing or a big blessing, it is our responsibility to do what is right with what God has given to each of us. As good stewards we tend to make better decisions with respect to giving. We must always be mindful that God looks at how we handle our blessings. We are showing our thanks and appreciation to our Heavenly Father when we are being good stewards.

If God has blessed you with a new home, make sure you take care of it. You should always keep in clean and neat. If you have been blessed with your business, you need to make sure you practice integrity and stand behind your value system. If you have been blessed with your ministry, you need to make sure you give it back to God. What I mean by this is that you should always let Him be in charge of what you do and what you say in this ministry because He is your leader. Your submission to God will help you to lead the flock with integrity and godly wisdom. If you have been blessed financially, you definitely don't want to be foolish with your money. The Bible says, "There is a treasure (wealth, something of great value) to be desired and oil in the dwelling of the wise; but a foolish man spendeth it up" (Proverbs 21:20).

BLESS THOSE WHO PURPOSELY REJECTED YOU

If you are thinking, "Why should I bless those who rejected me when I needed them? Why should I bless those who cursed me? Why should I bless those who used me? Why should I bless those who continue to mistreat me? Those questions are not hard to answer. What did Jesus say? He said, "But I say unto you, Love your enemies, bless them that curse you, do good to them that hate you, and pray for them which spitefully use you, and persecute you" (Matthew 5:44).

It would seem strange to feed a person who is hungry who did not feed you when you were hungry, right? It would seem awkward to give to someone who spoke bad things about you, right? And it would probably be difficult to even pray for someone who has wronged you, right? It just seems right to bless only the people who seemingly showed you love while you were in transition. But, Jesus said, "For if ye love them which love you, what reward have ye?" (Matthew 5:46). So, we will not get any brownie points with God by only loving certain people. We have to love everyone as Jesus did. We show love toward others through our actions.

Whenever God blesses you it is not for you to hold on to. No matter what type of blessing it is, you should be willing to release some of it. And no matter how someone has wronged you, it is always the godly thing to bless them in spite of what they have done. God said that He would make your enemy your footstool. (Psalm 110:1). I shared earlier about how badly Joseph's brothers treated him. God blessed Joseph exceedingly and he still blessed his brothers in spite of how they treated him.

INSPIRATION FOR YOUR HEART AND SOUL:
My sister, my brother, God saw fit to bless you with wealth, good health, a physical and spiritual promotion, and so many other things. I want to encourage you to be a blessing to someone else.I want to also encourage you not to be wasteful at all with your blessings.

PRAYER:
Lord, I thank you for blessing me beyond measure. I know that I can only look to you to bless me like this.

I pray that you will continue to pour your blessing upon me, my family, my friends and my enemies. I pray that you will bless me to be a good steward over my blessings. In Jesus name, Amen!

THOUGHT-PROVOKING QUESTIONS

Would you say that you are deserving of a harvest for your faithfulness? Do you have a heart of expectancy?

Do you believe that you are a good steward with your financial blessings? Have you ever mismanaged your finances? If so, do you remember some of the consequences you had to face as a result of mismanaging your finances?

Do you believe that it is right to bless people who rejected you? Do you believe that a person is selfish if they choose not to bless someone who rejected them?

TO CONTACT THE AUTHOR:
Yolanda Marshall
Email: victim2virtuous@gmail.com
www.yolandamarshall.com

Your testimony of how this book has helped to change your life is always welcomed. You may also want to consider reading, From Victim to Virtuous.

FROM

REJECTION

TO

RELATIONSHIP

WITH GOD

JOURNAL

*

_____

_____

_____

_____

_____

_____

_____

_____

_____

_____

_____

_____

_____

*

_____

_____

_____

_____

_____

_____

_____

_____

_____

_____

_____

_____

_____

_____

*

_____

_____

_____

_____

_____

_____

_____

_____

_____

_____

_____

_____

_____

*

_____

_____

_____

_____

_____

_____

_____

_____

_____

_____

_____

_____

FROM REJECTION TO RELATIONSHIP WITH GOD

*

*

_____

_____

_____

_____

_____

_____

_____

_____

_____

_____

_____

_____

_____

*

_____

_____

_____

_____

_____

_____

_____

_____

_____

_____

_____

_____

*

_____

_____

_____

_____

_____

_____

_____

_____

_____

_____

_____

_____

*

_____

_____

_____

_____

_____

_____

_____

_____

_____

_____

_____

_____

_____

_____

*

_____

_____

_____

_____

_____

_____

_____

_____

_____

_____

_____

_____

_____

_____

*

---

*

_____

_____

_____

_____

_____

_____

_____

_____

_____

_____

_____

_____

*

_____

_____

_____

_____

_____

_____

_____

_____

_____

_____

_____

_____

_____

*

_____

_____

_____

_____

_____

_____

_____

_____

_____

_____

_____

_____

*

_____

_____

_____

_____

_____

_____

_____

_____

_____

_____

_____

_____

_____

_____

*

----

*

_____

_____

_____

_____

_____

_____

_____

_____

_____

_____

_____

_____

_____

*

_____

_____

_____

_____

_____

_____

_____

_____

_____

_____

_____

_____

_____

*

_____

_____

_____

_____

_____

_____

_____

_____

_____

_____

_____

_____

_____

*

_____

_____

_____

_____

_____

_____

_____

_____

_____

_____

_____

_____

*

*

_____

_____

_____

_____

_____

_____

_____

_____

_____

_____

_____

_____

*

_____

_____

_____

_____

_____

_____

_____

_____

_____

_____

_____

_____

*

_____

_____

_____

_____

_____

_____

_____

_____

_____

_____

_____

_____

*

_____

_____

_____

_____

_____

_____

_____

_____

_____

_____

_____

_____

_____

*

_____

_____

_____

_____

_____

_____

_____

_____

_____

_____

_____

_____

*

_____

_____

_____

_____

_____

_____

_____

_____

_____

_____

_____

_____

_____

*

_____

_____

_____

_____

_____

_____

_____

_____

_____

_____

_____

_____

*

_____

_____

_____

_____

_____

_____

_____

_____

_____

_____

_____

_____

*

_____

_____

_____

_____

_____

_____

_____

_____

_____

_____

_____

_____

_____

*

---

*

_____

_____

_____

_____

_____

_____

_____

_____

_____

_____

_____

_____

_____

*

_____

_____

_____

_____

_____

_____

_____

_____

_____

_____

_____

_____

_____

*

_____

_____

_____

_____

_____

_____

_____

_____

_____

_____

_____

_____

*

_____

_____

_____

_____

_____

_____

_____

_____

_____

_____

_____

_____

_____

*

_____

_____

_____

_____

_____

_____

_____

_____

_____

_____

_____

_____

*

_____

_____

_____

_____

_____

_____

_____

_____

_____

_____

_____

_____

*

_____

_____

_____

_____

_____

_____

_____

_____

_____

_____

_____

_____

*

_____

_____

_____

_____

_____

_____

_____

_____

_____

_____

_____

_____

_____

_____

_____

_____

*

_____

_____

_____

_____

_____

_____

_____

_____

_____

_____

_____

_____

*

_____

_____

_____

_____

_____

_____

_____

_____

_____

_____

_____

_____

*

_____

_____

_____

_____

_____

_____

_____

_____

_____

_____

_____

_____

_____

*

_____

_____

_____

_____

_____

_____

_____

_____

_____

_____

_____

_____

_____

*

_____

_____

_____

_____

_____

_____

_____

_____

_____

_____

_____

_____

*

_____

_____

_____

_____

_____

_____

_____

_____

_____

_____

_____

_____

_____

_____

*

_____

_____

_____

_____

_____

_____

_____

_____

_____

_____

_____

_____

*

_____

_____

_____

_____

_____

_____

_____

_____

_____

_____

_____

_____

_____

_____

*

_____

_____

_____

_____

_____

_____

_____

_____

_____

_____

_____

_____

*

_____

_____

_____

_____

_____

_____

_____

_____

_____

_____

_____

_____

_____

_____

*

---

*

_____

_____

_____

_____

_____

_____

_____

_____

_____

_____

_____

_____

_____

_____

_____

FROM REJECTION TO RELATIONSHIP WITH GOD

*

---

*

_____

_____

_____

_____

_____

_____

_____

_____

_____

_____

_____

_____

_____

*

*

_____

_____

_____

_____

_____

_____

_____

_____

_____

_____

_____

_____

_____

*

_____

_____

_____

_____

_____

_____

_____

_____

_____

_____

_____

_____

*

_____

_____

_____

_____

_____

_____

_____

_____

_____

_____

_____

_____

_____

_____

*

_____

_____

_____

_____

_____

_____

_____

_____

_____

_____

_____

_____

_____

*

---

*

_____

_____

_____

_____

_____

_____

_____

_____

_____

_____

_____

_____

*

_____

_____

_____

_____

_____

_____

_____

_____

_____

_____

_____

_____

*

*

_____

_____

_____

_____

_____

_____

_____

_____

_____

_____

_____

_____

www.ingramcontent.com/pod-product-compliance
Lightning Source LLC
Chambersburg PA
CBHW020857090426
42736CB00008B/410